Life Is RELATIONSHIPS

Jaclynn Weber

© 2008
CHRISTIAN WOMANHOOD
8400 Burr Street
Crown Point, Indiana 46307
www.christianwomanhood.org
(219) 365-3202

ISBN-13: 978-0-9815087-1-9
ISBN-10: 0-9815087-1-5

CREDITS:
Layout and Cover Design: Mrs. Linda Stubblefield
Proofreaders: Mrs. Rena Fish, Mrs. Jane Grafton,
and Mrs. Cindy Schaap

Printed and Bound
in the United States

Dedication

$\mathscr{W}$hen I think of the two people who have most influenced my life, I immediately think of my parents, Jack and Cindy Schaap. They are really responsible for the writing of this book and my other books, and pretty much responsible for everything positive that has happened in my life.

I have an amazing heritage with four grandparents who are the greatest in the world; I have wonderful friends whom God has placed in my life and who have helped me follow the right path; I have an outstanding husband with whom I feel honored to share my life and who is a strong, godly leader in our home and who I love with all my heart; but the two people who have helped shape my life the most and who deserve more credit than I could ever give them in my lifetime are my parents.

It is through their years of love and training that I

have learned the importance of relationships and how to treat people. They are the ones who have taught me strong values and the importance of the home, the family, and the church. Through them I learned that people are more important than things and that everyone is equally important in God's eyes. They are the ones who taught me by their example as well as their words that God is real and should have first place in my life. They have taught me how to love God, my husband, and my children as well as the less fortunate, those overlooked by society, and yes, even my enemies.

My parents are my heroes, my role models, and my friends, and I love them with all of my heart. So as you read through this book, it is not really my words you are reading, but the training of two people who are, in my opinion, the greatest parents and teachers in the world.

Acknowledgments

$\mathscr{I}$ would like to thank Mrs. Linda Stubblefield for her countless hours of hard work and dedication to her job. She has been responsible for the putting together of each book I have written, not to mention the layout, cover design, and proofreading. She is definitely one of the hardest workers I know.

I would also like to thank Mrs. Rena Fish for her excellent job of proofreading as well as the following proofreaders: Mrs. Jane Grafton, Mrs. Cindy Schaap, and Mrs. Linda Stubblefield.

I would like to say a **huge** thank you to my friends, Sheri Dalton and Linda Tutton for not only helping me with the picture for the book cover, but for also being the best friends a girl could ask for. I love and admire you both.

A special thank you to Mr. Alex Midence for his photography.

Other Books by Jaclynn Weber

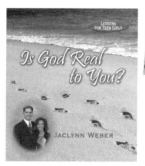

Table of Contents

Foreword

*W*hat an honor is mine to write a foreword to Jaclynn Weber's book on relationships. I ask, "Can one so young know this subject?" The answer comes, "Absolutely!"

I've watched my lovely granddaughter from childhood grow into a fine Christian lady with a husband and two children of her own. In every phase of her life, she tended to her primary relationship—her commitment to Jesus Christ. Because she keeps rightly related to Him Who is the source of love, she has related to others humbly and sacrificially.

The two great commandments found in Mark 12:30 and 31 are the secret to relationships. *"And thou shalt love the Lord thy God with all thy heart, and with all thy soul, and with all thy mind, and with all thy strength: this is the first commandment. And the second is like, namely this, Thou shalt love thy neighbour as thyself. There is none other*

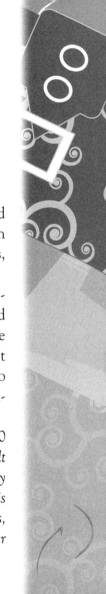

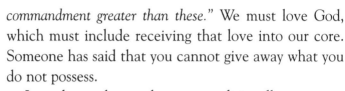

commandment greater than these." We must love God, which must include receiving that love into our core. Someone has said that you cannot give away what you do not possess.

In order to love others unconditionally, we must grasp the truth of how we are loved, yes, cherished, when not one deserves it. We learn, as Christ's followers, to love in the same way. Let Jaclynn's book speak to you on this vital subject. After all, the population of the entire world, with only one exception, is made up of others.

– Beverly Hyles

CHAPTER ONE

Life Is Relationships

Life is full of relationships:

- mother/daughter (son)
- father/daughter (son)
- brother/sister
- husband/wife
- grandparent/grandchild
- friend/friend
- boyfriend/girlfriend
- employer/employee

These are just a few of the relationships that people can have during their lifetime. When these and other relationships are going well and everyone is getting along, life is wonderful. However, when one of these relationships is broken and people are at odds with each other, life can seem very depressing and bitter.

What is a major cause of teenage depression and suicide? "He broke up with me" or "I just can't go on without her." Often when parents cannot get along and instead divorce, the kids blame themselves, and they see no way out except by putting a gun to their head. How did that begin? By a broken relationship.

The Bible tells us that when our ways are pleasing to God, even our enemies will be at peace with us, and He tells us in Romans 12:18, *"If it be possible, as much as lieth in you, live peaceably with all men."*

There are many, many examples of people in the Bible who succeeded in life because of good relationships, and there are those who struggled because they had trouble getting along with someone:

- Queen Esther saved the lives of her people because she had a great relationship with her cousin and her husband, the king.

- Judas committed suicide because he could not live with the fact that he had accepted 30 pieces of silver to betray Jesus.

- King Saul had a miserable ending to his life because he was so jealous of David.

- God blessed Ruth and gave her Boaz for a husband because she loved and obeyed her mother-in-law.

- Samson had his eyes plucked out and became a slave because his girlfriend lied to him and betrayed him.

These are just a few of the many stories of real people who lived long ago in a very different world than the one in which we live today. Yet, the principles and relationship struggles and victories with which they dealt are exactly the same as we have today.

There was a teenage girl with whom I went to school, and for a while, I could not seem to get along with her. She was older than I was, and she was a "say-what-you-think" type of person. She did not seem to be afraid of anyone or anything, but I was afraid of her.

Well, she did not like me for some reason (can you imagine that?!) and would not speak to me for several months unless she absolutely had to. We were put in a situation where we had to be together for something on a regular basis, and those times were not very com-

fortable—to say the least. During that time in my life, I learned that when you are not getting along with someone, it affects your whole life. In time, that relationship healed itself; but sometimes, no matter how hard we try to "fix" it, it will not be fixed. Sometimes we need to back off, pray about it, and give the relationship time to heal. Broken people are not like broken toys: you do not replace the batteries and five minutes later they're working like new again. Relationships take weeks, months, and often even a few years to heal and start "working" again.

The Bible says that we should get along with people to the best of our ability. Even Paul, the great Apostle, wrote *"If it be possible,…live peacably with all men."* Sometimes you cannot help the fact that someone just does not like you for whatever reason.

I like a statement that my Grandpa Hyles used to make. "I may offend people because of my position, but I never want to offend people because of my disposition." Some people may not like the fact that I am a preacher's daughter or that I was chosen to receive an honor they felt they deserved, but I never want anyone to hate me because I was a snob or I treated

someone like he was not important. Jesus died for those who don't like me as much as He died for my closest friends. He loves everyone, and so should I. That does not mean that everyone will be my closest friend, and I may not particularly enjoy being around certain people, but I should treat them with the same kindness and the same love that Jesus showed when He stretched out His arms on the tree and said, "Father, forgive them; for they know not what they do."

Life is relationships. Is there one on which you need to work? Start today!

CHAPTER TWO

The Mother-Daughter Relationship

"Honour thy father and mother; which is the first commandment with promise." (Ephesians 6:2)

A mother is there when:

>...you need someone to talk to.
>...you don't feel like talking to anyone.

>...you have a great victory.
>...you suffer a horrible defeat.

>...you have your first real date!
>...your boyfriend breaks your heart.

>...you take your first step.
>...you fall down and skin your knee.

…you finally receive your driver's license.
…you wreck your car.

…you are feeling on top of the world.
…you wish you could drop off the end of the earth.

…you feel like laughing uncontrollably.
…your tears won't stop falling.

…you need advice.
…you want to make your own decisions.

…you come home from the hospital after being born.
…you walk down the aisle on your wedding day and leave home forever.

…when you need her.
…when you think you don't (and you really do).

Please let me ask you some questions about your relationship with your mom.

- When is the last time you thanked your mom for being there for you?

- When was the last time you told your mom you love her?

- What was the last thing you said to her when you left her to go to school this morning?

- When was the last time you did something with her that she wanted to do?

Every good relationship takes time and effort, and the mother/daughter relationship is no exception. In fact, as you become a teenager and young adult, it takes extra time and effort if you want to be close and get along.

Everyone told me this, but I never completely understood it until I looked in the face of my own daughter Lyndsay for the first time. "When you have your own child someday," they would say, "you will appreciate your mom like never before," and I found out how true that statement is.

My mom and I always had a good relationship when I was growing up, but during my teen years, it became a little harder to get along. I was becoming more of a woman, less of a little girl. I had opinions

(sometimes very strong ones!), and I was not very shy about stating them. My mom very wisely let me "state my opinions" until I calmed down and had talked everything out. By the time she was done listening, she usually had talked some sense into me! She was (and still is) a wonderful mom, a good listener, and my dearest friend. Now that I have a daughter of my own, I love and admire her even more.

My purpose for writing this article, though, is really not to give you a lot of pointers on how to be a good daughter or lecture about all of the ways you are failing as a daughter. (I am sure you are all wonderful daughters and love your moms very much.) Like I wrote at the beginning, a mother is the person who is always there for you, who loves you unconditionally, and who believes in you with all of her heart—no matter what you do. She is also the person who is the easiest to take for granted because she is always there. So often we see her as the taxi driver, the house cleaner, the cook, the chaperon, and the laundromat attendant because, of course, she is supposed to do all of those things, but we often fail to thank her and give her the praise that she deserves. We fail to see the

tired eyes, the gnarled hands, the love on her face for us, the tears she cries privately because she longs to be close to us—to show us somehow just how much she loves us. We go through our days busy with our own lives—never taking time to notice the one to whom we owe our lives—the one who helped bring us into the world (and who sometimes reminds us that she can "take us out" too!)

My friend and her mom are very close. They are the best of friends, and even though they live quite far apart, they talk to each other and spend as much time together as possible. She always thought, like many of us are prone to do, that her mom would be healthy and strong forever. One day her mom began feeling sick. When she went to the doctor, she learned that she had a very serious form of cancer. She, her mom, and her family cried and prayed for God to work a miracle, but God does not always answer like we want Him to, and she underwent extensive chemo and radiation treatment. Finally, her cancer went into remission, and the family was so excited. However, their excitement vanished when last year the doctors found her cancer had returned, and her days on earth are limited unless God chooses to miraculously heal her.

Even though my friend does not know how long she will have her mother on earth, she can have peace in knowing that 1) she will see her mother in Heaven and 2) she has developed a strong relationship with her mother that will outlast any trial or disappointment or illness that comes their way. The truth is, if my friend's mother were to pass away tonight and she never spoke to her again, my friend would live the rest of her life being able to say "I'm glad I did" instead of "I wish I had."

Can you say the same for your relationship with your mom? If you were the friend in this story and your mom was the one dying of cancer, would you be able first of all to say that you will see her in Heaven? Secondly, is your relationship so strong that nothing would be able to tear you apart, or would there be some major pleas for forgiveness and tears of regret and remorse for things you wish you could take back and redo? I know we all tend to think "that will never happen to me," but then it does. How are you preparing if that day were to come to you?

Allow me close this chapter with some of the same questions I asked earlier in this chapter:

- When is the last time you thanked your mom for being there for you?

- When did you last tell your mom you love her?

- What was the last thing you said to your mom before you walked out the door?

- When was the last time you did something with her that she wanted to do?

I believe I will let my mom know today how much I love and appreciate her. What about you?

CHAPTER THREE

But She's Not My Mom!

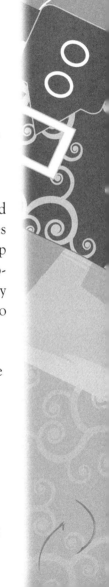

"*But* she's not my mom!" I have heard people make this statement and other similar ones when talking about how to have a good relationship with their stepparents. Though I have never had a stepparent, those I have talked to who have one and my friends who have had one say it can be very difficult to get along with a stepparent.

I recently asked several ladies at our church to speak to the teens at our ladies' conference. Since one of them came from a split home, I asked her if she would speak on how to have a good relationship with a stepfather. She called me back and said she did not feel qualified to speak on that subject. She said, "My stepdad was closer to me than my real dad, and I never even think of his being a stepparent. He has loved me and taken care of me for as long as I can remember, and I consider him my father. I don't think

I would do a good job speaking on that subject because I do not have the typical stepparent situation." She spoke on a different subject, and I was intrigued to hear her say how much she loved her stepfather.

A girl came to me several years ago asking me how she could deal with the bitterness in her heart toward her stepfather. She said, "I don't know why I have to listen to him; he's not my 'real' dad!"

Her stepdad is a godly man who loves her and her family very much. I told her that God had put a godly man in her life who loved her and would help guide her through her teenage years if she would let him. I said, "You will never love him as you love your own father; there will always be a special place in your heart for your birth dad. You can have a good relationship with your stepdad, though, and love him too. He is not there to replace the relationship with your birth father; he is there to love you and guide you as only he can do." She is a great girl who today, I believe, has a good relationship with her stepdad.

One of my friends in college was from a split home, and both parents had remarried. She got along well with her stepdad and mom, but her stepmom was jealous of her and just did not like her very much. It was very difficult for my friend. She did not know what to do, so she got some advice from a counselor who told her to start doing things for her stepmom to help her to love her. You see, love is action, and the more you do things for people to express your love, the more you will love them.

Anyway, she began writing her notes, calling her, sending her gifts and cards, and slowly the stepmother became kinder and more accepting of my friend. She realized her stepdaughter was not a threat to her; my friend just did not know how to handle having a "new" mom. Now, they are not as close as she and her birth mom are, but they have a good relationship because someone decided to do the best she could with the situation she was in.

The stepparent/stepchild relationship is not a natural relationship like husband-wife, father-son, or mother-daughter. Yet, it can be a positive and close relationship, but like many things in life, much depends on your attitude. If you decide you hate your stepmom and nothing she does is going to change that fact,

then you and she probably will never get along. But if you decide that you are going to try to love and accept this person who has been suddenly put in your life, then your home will be a much more peaceful place, and you might even have a good relationship with your stepparent! (That would really be going overboard!) We cannot control what God brings into our lives, but we can control how we react to it.

If 50 percent of American marriages end in divorce, then many of you reading this article probably have a stepparent. I wish no teenager ever had to experience the rejection felt by a parent's walking out of the home. That is a major cause of teenage suicide. But let me ask you, "Once you get past the anger, the bitterness, and the feelings of rejection, what are you doing about your relationship with your stepparent?"

- Is it unfair? Yes.
- Was this your choice? No.
- Do you want to listen to your stepparent? Probably not.

But like it or not, that person is there, and there's not a whole lot you can do about that. You can decide, though, to make your home and your life

"hell" on earth with "World War III" happening every day, or you can choose to love and accept the stepparent and have "heaven" on earth. What will you choose?

CHAPTER FOUR

Honor Thy Father

The relationship you have with your father determines the kind of relationship you will have with your husband. I love to see my daughter Lyndsay playing with my husband. He loves to spend time with her when he comes home from work, and sometimes he takes her out on "dates." She worships the ground he walks on, and he is her idol and hero. There is something in her that is instilled in all of us, and her obvious love and desire for acceptance from her daddy is like looking into a mirror of my childhood.

From the time we are barely able to walk, God puts within each of us a strong desire to feel accepted by a man. That desire begins with loving a daddy as a little girl and wanting to marry him when we grow up, and the need for acceptance grows until we are women and want acceptance and love from another man— our husband.

It is so vital that we develop a close, loving relationship with our father because that is the foundation for a deep, long-lasting marriage to a husband some day. Many teenage girls (and even adult women) struggle with not feeling accepted and instead feel insecure because they do not have a good relationship with their father or do not have a strong, loving father who loves them and leads the home. These girls often try to cover up their feelings with dating lots of guys. This is the kind of girl who is always in a serious relationship, and when one boy breaks up with her, she immediately is on the rebound for another relationship.

First of all, to those of you who have a strong, loving father at home, I cannot stress this enough: develop a good relationship with him!!

- Thank God daily for your dad.

- Write him notes often.

- Take every opportunity you have to be with him.

- Ask him to take you and your friends out.

- Leave messages on his cell phone when he is busy, telling him you miss him.

- Tell him at least once every day that you love him.

- Go on dates with him. You are never "too old" to go on dates with your dad! (I still do!)

- Give him backrubs.

- Tell him your feelings.

- Let him approve the guys you date and be involved in the relationship because he cares more than you know.

These are just a few of the ways to be close to your dad.

The relationship you have with your father determines the kind of relationship you will have with your husband. To those of you who do not have a godly, loving father at home, first of all be good to your father and never criticize him. If he is an alcoholic, a drug addict, or a homeless man who lives on the street, NEVER criticize him. If he is a deacon or a staff

member who acts godly at church but is ungodly at home, NEVER criticize him.

If it is at all possible for you to be close to your father, then I beg you, please do it. In many cases, however, a girl does not have the opportunity like I had to be close to her dad, yet she needs desperately to feel loved and accepted by a man in her life.

To those of you who do not have the opportunity to be close to your dad, I would strongly encourage you to be close to your pastor, your youth pastor, or a strong male leader in your church. No, I do not mean go live with them at their house, sit with them in every service, or follow them around everywhere. The only person who can truly take the place of a missing father in the home is your Heavenly Father, Jesus Christ.

However, you do need someone on earth (with "skin on him") to lead you and guide you and to help you make wise decisions. Ask him for advice before making any big decisions in your life—whom to date, college choices, job opportunities, etc. You also need someone who will help you be able to make wise decisions, and men are much more rational and natural

problem solvers than are we "emotional" women.

Lastly, let me address those of you who have been or are being abused physically, emotionally, or sexually. Please go to a godly person and get help immediately. The only exception to "Children obey your parents" occurs when the parents are telling you to disobey God. Then and only then are you allowed (and encouraged) to tell someone and help your parents to see that what they are telling you to do is wrong. Don't "survive" abuse and let things go on that will affect you emotionally forever. God loves you, and He does not want you to be hurt. My desire is that every girl reading this would have a close, wonderful father-daughter relationship, and remember, "the relationship you have with your father determines the relationship you have with your husband." Let me add the following: it also determines the relationship you have with your Heavenly Father.

CHAPTER FIVE

I Wish You Were My Dad

When I was younger, my dad and I started a bus route in East Chicago, Indiana. Every week we would go visiting for several hours; then early Sunday morning, we would pick up the kids.

I made many friends through the years of working on Dad's bus, and many of them did not have fathers living at home. Often, one of them would ride our bus and say to me, "You are so lucky. I wish I had a dad like you have. I wish Brother Jack was my dad."

I felt so sorry for them, and it also made me thankful for the father God gave me.

I attended a funeral recently for a man whose kids went to school with me. The man who passed away was my dad's age, and I couldn't help but wonder while I looked into the solemn face of the man who was now in Heaven, "What if that had been my dad?"

I have been so blessed and so privileged to have

had a strong, loving father throughout my 26 years of living. Whenever I need fatherly counsel or advice, I have the security of knowing that he is just a phone call away.

At this writing, I am reading a book about the 9/11 tragedy, and it describes a family whose father died in the Twin Towers, leaving a wife and son to grieve him alone. However, the saddest part was not the loss of the father, but the fact that the eight-year-old son felt no loss because he barely knew him. His father was always too busy for him with his work, and he had sacrificed a close, loving relationship for power and for money.

I also was blessed to have a wonderful father who always made time for me. If it meant not making quite as much money as he could have or not being as rec-ognized around the country as he would have been, he chose spending time with his family. I knew Dad loved me more than his wallet and cared for us more than he cared about his own reputation and what people would think.

I wish so much that every girl in the world could grow up with a strong, loving father like I had. I wish everyone could feel the security and acceptance that my daughter Lyndsay already feels and receives from my husband.

This year several of the girls in my Sunday school class do not have their dad living at home. One girl's father is in Vietnam, one girl's father passed away, several of the girls have parents who are divorced, and some do not even know where their dad is.

To those girls and to all of you who do not have a loving, caring father like I have, please open your heart and allow me to give you a few words of comfort and security.

1. Remember that God loves you, and He will always be your Father. I have heard the Ron Hamiltons (Patch the Pirate) sing a song called "Abba, Father," and the words to the chorus are as follows:

"Abba, Father, I trust in You,

You're always faithful; You're always true...."

If your father walked out on you, God will always be here for you. If your father makes promises and never comes through on his word, God never falters or fails. "...*I will never thee, nor forsake thee.*" (Hebrews 13:5)

God promised to take us to Heaven if we ask Him, and He promises to be with us when we go through our darkest valleys. He is never too busy or too preoccupied, and He wants to be with you more than you could ever know.

2. Trust Him with every decision you make. No, your dad may not be available for advice, but God's Word has all of the guidance and instruction that we need; all we have to do is look for it!

May I encourage those of you without a father at home to study your Bible, write down what certain verses mean to you, and memorize God's Word. You never know when you will need a certain verse to get you through a difficult day.

3. Use your pastor as your sounding board and decision maker. Especially those whose fathers are gone, but also those with godly fathers in the home, should seek wisdom and advice from their pastor before making any major decision.

I remember going to my Papaw Hyles, who was my pastor, for advice one time after I had already made my decision. I really did not want advice at the time—just approval. Well, I did get advice, but not approval. He told me, "Jaclynn, if you would have come to me six months ago and asked me about that, I would have told you not to do it, but it is already done."

How unwise I had been not to go to my pastor first.

4. If you have been hurt by a father in any way, don't blame all men. Don't get bitter and decide to stay an old maid the rest of your life because your dad did not treat you right.

All men and women are created equal, but some abuse the gifts God has given them, and many times innocent people are hurt deeply by their foolish decisions. God loves you—period. Don't question why; just trust Him, and He will direct your path.

If you trust God, seek His wisdom, and let your pastor guide, then I fully believe each of you will one day find true love, peace, and happiness with the wonderful, loving husband and family God has chosen for you.

CHAPTER SIX

Do You Love Your Brother?

*P*roverbs 17:17 says, *"A friend loveth at all times, and a brother is born for adversity."* I think the last part of this verse was my motto in my relationship with my brother when I was a little girl as we would argue over stupid things and tell on each other. As we grew older, however, we developed more of a friend relationship as we realized we loved each other, were "stuck" with each other, and yes, at times, even needed each other. Now as an adult, though I do not get to spend a lot of time with my brother, there is nothing I would not do for him, and I consider him not only my brother, but also a friend whom I respect and I admire.

Corrie ten Boom was a teenager at the time of Hitler's attack against the Jewish people. She and her family hid many Jewish refugees in a "secret" room in their house, located above their watch shop. One day the German soldiers came unexpectedly and found the refugees. Corrie, along with her family and the Jews, was sent to a concentration camp. Corrie had a sister who was her best friend, and they were separated for awhile. One day after months of Corrie's thinking she would never again see her beloved sister, her sister arrived, looking very thin and frail, at the same concentration camp. Corrie was so thrilled to see her sister again, and she now felt a glimmer of hope midst all of the depression and pain.

Through the weeks and months of beatings, starvation, surviving the gas chambers and the constant humiliation, the two sisters encouraged each other as well as the others in the camp. Lice epidemics would sweep through the cabins, and they would shave each other's heads. If one was sick, the other would give up her food for that day—even though they both were near starvation. They stayed up at night huddled together singing and asking God to help them.

Corrie's sister began to weaken slowly from exhaustion, starvation, and sickness. Her body became diseased from the filthy conditions and malnutrition, and she began to waste away to nothing. Corrie was heartbroken, and she did her best to nurse her sister back

to health, but it was no use. There simply was nothing she could do. One morning as the military did their routine wake-up call, Corrie awakened to find her beloved sister dead. She was now truly alone—without any family—and she barely survived the next few months in that sordid place.

Finally the Germans surrendered, and Corrie was freed. She soon discovered that she was the only one in her family who did not die in the camps. She later wrote the book *The Hiding Place* in which she shares her incredible story.

I wonder sometimes, as we fight and argue with each other over the seemingly unimportant things in our lives, what would happen if we were ever placed in a situation like Corrie's. Do we really love each other but never show it, or are we too self-centered to care about our own family whom God put in our household? If we as Christians were ever attacked and tortured for our beliefs as the Jews were, most of the things we argue with each other about would matter less than one small speck of sand falling into the ocean. For when we look at the whole picture of our lives, the most important "things" are the people God has placed in them. People are always more important than things, and when we place more value on something we think we must have than we do on the person who has it or gave it to us, we have overlooked what truly matters.

Your sister means more than the sweater she borrowed (or stole!) from you. That brother is too important for you to criticize or put down and call a bother when he hangs around you and your friends. Your little sister's life is far too precious to be influenced by the rock music you play when she is in your car. I want to ask you, do you realize the influence you have on your little sister? In many ways you hold her life in your hands to either crush or mold into something great. She wants to be like you, so are you worthy of copying?

I always wished while growing up that I had a sister. I thought it would be so fun to share secrets, trade clothes, and talk about "girl things" with her! Obviously, I never had a sister, but God has given me four sisters-in-law whom I love very much. Three of them, Sandra, Angie, and Chelsey, live far away, and I always enjoy being with them and wish I could see

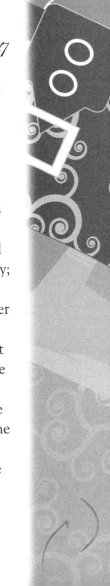

them more. My brother's wife, Candace, lives only 15 minutes away, and she is one of the nicest people in the whole world. Although she has five sisters of her own, she has been so kind and loving to me, and I consider her a close friend. I would do anything for her. I am so glad we have a good relationship, and I am also thankful that my brother and I grew closer as we got older and developed a good relationship. If things got bad and times were hard, I know we would be there for each other because we are not only family; we have become friends.

You may not have been able to choose that brother or sister who is sometimes so annoying and irritating, but you can choose to make him or her your friend. It may not seem important now, but one day you may be another Corrie Ten Boom, and that sister may be all you have in the world. Let's look at the whole picture and focus on the beautiful seashore instead of that one pesky little grain of sand. Have you ever heard the motto "my sister—my friend"? Well, that can become your motto, and I challenge you to make it yours.

CHAPTER SEVEN

I Love My Grandparents

In my opinion, my grandparents are the youngest looking and youngest acting grandparents in the world. I have so many fun memories of each of them.

I remember riding on the back of my great-grandpa's motorcycle as we went speeding down the highway, thinking, "My great-grandpa is **so** cool!"

My Papaw Hyles, as we called him, never seemed old even before the day he died. When I was younger, I would ride home with him from church on Sunday morning. When he was in the car, he would slouch way down in his seat, pull his glasses down over his nose, and start swerving all over the road like a "crazy" driver. I would laugh and laugh, and I loved being with him.

I remember one birthday when he surprised me by showing up at the door of my grade school classroom

and called me out of class. I went out to see him, and he handed me a whole stack of McDonald's coupons and wished me "Happy Birthday!" I felt so special that day.

I remember playing "Guesstures" with my Grandma Hyles, who is one of the most beautiful ladies I know, and watching her get on the floor on all fours and start crawling like a dog so we would guess her word in time! That was a mental picture I'll never forget!

We've had many ski trips with my Grandpa Schaap as well as lots of winters sledding behind the truck at his house over Christmas. I remember one time when my dad, my grandpa, and I were all on the same ski lift together. It was almost time to get off, and as we said, "Ready, set, go," Dad and I skied off, but when we turned around, Grandpa was still going around the lift! I guess he got nervous, so he jumped off the lift through the air and landed in a pile of snow! We thought he might be hurt, but he got right up, brushed himself off, and skied down the hill!

Grandma Schaap is one of the most loving, fun people I know! Last year my two children and I went to Florida for a week to see my grandma because they live there during the winter months.

My friend from college days, Heidi Carrillo, lives near where my grandparents live so we decided to get together. Grandma, who loves ice cream, took us to her favorite ice cream store for lunch. We each ordered a huge sundae, then we shopped, took the kids to the park, and stayed downtown the whole day. By the time the get-together was finished and after Grandma had spoiled Heidi, me, and our kids rotten, we got ready to leave, and Heidi said, "I love your Grandma Schaap! She's the most fun grandma ever!" I agree with her, and I love being with Grandma Schaap.

I could go on and on about exciting trips to Texas with Grandma Hyles, about girls' nights with Papaw Hyles in college (One night I disguised myself, walked up to him, and kissed him on the cheek. He slapped me because he did not know who I was!), of trips with Grandma and Grandpa Schaap, and many great times we have had together. They have been so good to me, yet sometimes it has been easy to take them for granted.

On February 6, 2001, when we found out that my

Grandpa Hyles did not make it through his heart surgery and was in Heaven, all of a sudden those memories of times we spent together were very precious to me. I realized then how fortunate I was to have had such wonderful grandparents.

I remember when my cousin Tami Parks was in college and we received a phone call that our great-grandmother was dying. She picked me up from school, and we drove to Holland, Michigan, to see her before she passed away.

These people in my life are very special to me, and when they are all gone someday (hopefully many, many years from now), all I will have left are the memories I made with them. It will not matter what they leave me or how much "stuff" I received from them. The relationship I had with them and the wonderful times we shared will last a lifetime.

The truths they have taught me through their lives as well as through their children will live on long after they are gone through me and my children, and hopefully, for many generations to follow. The Bible says in Psalm 16:6, *"The lines are fallen unto me in pleasant places; yea, I have a goodly heritage."* There is so much we can learn from the good (and even bad) decisions made by those who are older than we are. I want to learn everything I can from those whom God has placed in my life.

You may be reading this and thinking, "My grandparents are not very fun. They are stuffy, boring, grouchy, old people. I don't like to be around them!"

Well, have you ever asked them about their past or how they grew up? Many of them probably lived through the Depression, and maybe some of them even fought in a war. Not all of them have had as easy of a life as you and I have had, and I bet they would love to sit down with you and tell you "all about it"! Well, why don't you let them?

When I was in high school, one of my teachers, Mrs. Jeanine Nelson, had each of us interview our grandparents as a class assignment, and I was shocked how much I learned from my grandparents! It was fun hearing their stories and learning about their past.

If your grandparents are alive and well today, thank God for them and decide you are going to learn all you can and spend as much time with them as possible while they are here. They are not getting

younger, and though it may not sound as exciting as talking to your boyfriend on the phone, one day (not too far away for some), you will look one last time at their body before their casket is lowered into the ground and all you will have left is the time you spent with them and the memories you have made. Don't wait until it is too late to find out what amazing people they were!

CHAPTER EIGHT

Friends Forever

Proverbs 18:24, "*A man that hath friends must shew himself friendly....*"

A girl and her friend are arm-in-arm on the playground of their elementary school, playing, laughing, and talking about "secret" things—the color of their hair ribbons, which boy has the most "cooties," what the new girl is like, why the dog got sick, etc.—important things! As they skip around and play jump rope or tag, they have no thoughts of their future, who they will marry or what trials and heartaches life may hold. They are happy in each other's company, and I cannot help but think that God looks down and wishes we would always have that innocent, open spirit with Him and also each other.

It is unbelievable how cruel and hateful those same sweet girls can become toward each other in junior high and high school. As they start to notice boys and

become old enough to date, they often exchange a lifelong friendship for a relationship with a boy who many times will come and be gone within a month.

What happens to those sweet young girls who vow on the playground to be "best friends" forever? Let's take a look and see what God has to say about how we treat our friends. In Proverbs 18:24 the Bible tells us that if we want to have friends, we must first be a friend.

Many lonely people in this world are waiting for someone to reach out and be their friend, but the Bible says that it is our job to be a friend. The friendlier and kinder we are to those around us, the more friends we are likely to have. Are you being a friend to someone, or are you constantly looking for someone to be a friend to you?

The Bible also talks about the friendship of Jonathan and David and how the bond they shared between them was so strong that nothing could destroy it. The Bible says that the love Jonathan had for David was "*...passing the love of women.*" Now, there was nothing "odd" or "strange" about their relationship; they were just two friends who were there for each other even if it cost them their lives.

My Grandpa Hyles used to say that you were very fortunate to meet one true friend in your lifetime. Many friends and friendships come and go like the changing of the seasons. In high school you can get so close you think you will never drift apart; in junior high your best friend changes weekly, sometimes daily; in college you live with each other and learn to love and accept each other's flaws, ups and downs, and you grow very close. Yet even those friends finish college, leave, and sometimes are never to be heard from again.

I do believe God sends friendships into our lives at different times for different reasons. I had a group of friends in high school whom I know God sent to me because they helped me stay out of trouble and become a better person.

When I was in college, a lot of people liked me because I was Dr. Hyles' granddaughter or Dr. Schaap's daughter, and God sent some friends into my life who did not care what my name was and who liked me for me, and we became very close.

I tend to be a very analytical, anxious, sometimes

worried person, and I believe God had sent some very fun-loving, godly people into my life to keep me from becoming too serious about life. You know, we are supposed to have fun serving the Lord, not be depressed and down all the time. Who wants to be around a sad person? Those friends truly are gifts from God.

So what are you doing about being a friend? How are your relationships with your friends? Are you using them to get something from them? Are you only their friend if they are yours? Are you only kind to those in "your group"?

In closing, let me give you just a few ideas on how to have a great relationship with your friends.

1. Be friendly to everyone, but be very cautious when choosing close friends. Choose friends who help you become a better person. Don't pick "mission projects" for friends.

2. Look for ways to help your friends. Don't look for ways they can help you.

3. Be quick to give, but slow to borrow! *"The liberal* [giving] *soul shall be made fat: and he that watereth* [gives] *shall be watered* [have his needs cared for] *also himself."* (Proverbs 11:25)

4. Don't put your friends on trial. If a person is your friend, enjoy that friendship and don't analyze every day whether or not that person still likes you. Remember, everyone has good days and bad days, so give your friend some space.

5. Apologize if you have hurt your friend or even think you might have hurt her. I would rather apologize a hundred times and keep a friendship than lose one because I was too stubborn to say, "I'm sorry."

I hope these ideas will help you make friends and strengthen the relationships with the friends you have. May you and your friends truly be "best friends forever."

CHAPTER NINE

Who Could Love That Person?

$\mathscr{I}$ used to wonder when I worked on my dad's bus route why God gave me the life I have and the kids on the bus the lives they had. I would say in my heart, "Why did God put me in a loving home with two parents who love each other and where I have all the things I could want or need, and many of these children do not know where their father is, and they do not even have the basic things they need. Why do I sleep in a nice, warm bed, and they sleep on a mattress in the living room? Why do they have to live in roach- and rat-infested houses, and I live in a home that is always spotless?" The only time we ever saw a mouse in the house, we called 9-1-1! (We thought someone had broken into our house and was going through some bags in the base-

ment. When the police came and found a mouse, my mother and I felt really stupid!)

If God is the loving, kind, just, fair God that I know He is, then why does He allow some people to suffer and go through so much pain and others to seemingly have "the easy life"? My dad once said that he is not surprised when bad things happen to people; he is surprised when good things happen to any of us. We are all sinners; we all deserve Hell; we all disappoint God, so anything good He does for us is because of His grace (giving us what we do not deserve).

How Do You Treat People?

Your relationship with those less fortunate than yourself is one of life's most important relationships. How you treat those who are poor, sick, old, handicapped, and helpless shows a lot about who you really are on the inside. Jesus talks over and over again about the importance of treating the poor and needy with kindness.

- *"This poor man cried, and the LORD heard him, and saved him out of all his troubles."* (Psalm 34:6)

- *"...he that hath mercy on the poor, happy is he."* (Proverbs 14:21)
- *"Whoso mocketh the poor reproacheth his Maker...."* (Proverbs 17:5)
- *"The rich and poor meet together: the* LORD *is the maker of them all."* (Proverbs 22:2)
- *"Rob not the poor, because he is poor: neither oppress the afflicted in the gate."* (Proverbs 22:22)

These are just a few of the verses that address God's love and compassion on the poor and the needy.

My Grandpa Hyles used to say, "How could one ball of dirt say to another ball of dirt, 'You are worthless'?" They are both the same in God's eyes.

A girl in my Sunday school class started coming this year during the fall program. She is a very sweet girl, but she is deformed. If you were to look at her face, it looks as if someone took it and smashed it into her skull. Her fingers are only half the size of average fingers, and she cannot hold things very well. She obviously does not have anyone at home who loves her enough to take care of her because she smells very bad when she comes to class, and her hair is always greasy and stringy. If you saw Deanna, you would

probably think, "That poor girl; she looks awful."

I've heard my dad say that if God were going to test us and see how well we treat people, He would probably come to earth dressed like a homeless person—someone whom most of the world would reject.

I think God put Deanna in my class because she needed someone to care about her and love her. She needs someone to teach her how to bathe, wash her hair, clean her clothes, and smell nice. She also needs to feel loved and accepted by someone. If I don't love her and help her and if the girls in my class do not make her feel accepted, then who will?

Our church is often called "The Church With a Heart," and if people like Deanna come and do not feel loved, then where else can they go? The world is going to toss them to the side, and most people would not even want to look at them—much less stop and help them.

In my dad's book *What to Expect in the Pursuit of God*, he tells the story about a young man with six-inch-long arms, no elbows, and three little protrusions for fingers. My dad met Chris at a camp and tells about seeing him get dressed one morning. He watched in amazement as Chris put on his shirt by placing the shirt on the floor, lying down on it, and wiggling his arms until he got them in the sleeves. Then he stood up and adjusted his shirt by leaning against the wall. He did ask my dad to button it for him. He put an apparatus with a clamp on it in his mouth to put on his socks and shoes. He stuck his feet in his shoes and used his tongue, his lips, and his teeth to tie the laces. My dad wrote that it was amazing to watch Chris in action.

A college student who was there with my dad asked if he could borrow the car to go to town. He wanted to buy Chris some new shoes. He chose some shoes with Velcro closures. When my dad and the college student presented Chris with the shoes, he wept. When he put on the shoes, it took him only two minutes instead of more than a half hour! Dad wrote about how Chris was so thrilled.

You know, I think God was quite pleased with that college student who, instead of making fun of Chris, decided to accept him and help in whatever way he could.

The way we treat the poor, the needy, the elderly,

and the helpless really shows how good of a Christian we are. It is easy for all of us, and especially teenagers, to become selfish and feel like we deserve to have the best and that everyone else should plan his life around us.

The best way to cure this problem is by getting on a bus route, visiting a nursing home, or going to see someone who has been hospitalized for several weeks or months. Take a gift to an elderly person at church and watch his/her face light up when the realization hits that someone still cares.

The greatest test of your Christianity and love for God is not just found in standing up in a huge auditorium singing "Stand up for Jesus" in front of a crowd of atheists, though that would take courage. Your spirituality is not measured by how much Bible you can quote for an audience. Your greatness is determined simply by this: how do you treat those who are less fortunate than you? How much do you love those who can give you nothing in return? Jesus says this is the true measure of greatness.

CHAPTER TEN

My Enemy ~ My Friend

Have you ever had a person in your life who you knew did not like you? I am not talking about someone who was jealous of you or who was not one of your closest friends. I mean, have you ever had someone who you felt was trying to ruin your reputation and do everything in his or her power to hurt you? If you have ever been in that situation, then you know how hard and hurtful it can be.

I have only had a couple of people in my life that I felt have ever really disliked me, and the couple of times I have been through that, do you know what I have wanted to do? I wanted to walk right up to the person, tell the person exactly what I thought about him or her, and then punch the person in the face as hard as I could! Now, I never actually did that! I just felt like doing that!

Unfortunately, my thoughts and feelings were

exactly opposite of how the Bible says we are to treat our enemies. In Proverbs 16:7 the Bible says, *"When a man's ways please the Lord, he maketh even his enemies to be at peace with him."*

Proverbs 25:21 says, *"If thine enemy be hungry, give him bread to eat; and if he be thirsty, give him water to drink."*

Matthew 5:44 says, *"...Love your enemies, bless them that curse you, do good to them that hate you, and pray for them which despitefully use you, and persecute you."* (Read Matthew 5:43-48)

One of the things I admire the most about my dad, who is also my pastor, is that he lives these verses, and he does his best to treat his enemies like God would treat them. I once heard someone say, "If you never do anything great in life, then you will never have any enemies." Anytime you decide to take a stand and do right, there will be people who will try to stop you and pull you down to their level.

Jesus even says, *"...Vengeance is mine; I will repay...."* (Romans 12:19) When we have those feelings of wanting to get even and hurt the ones who have hurt us, we must remember that God said He will take care of them for us, and it is His job alone to do so.

As a teenager, many hurtful and vicious things can be said about someone who does not deserve such hatred. Many people (because they are insecure or jealous) lash out at those who they feel are better than they are, hoping they will feel better about themselves. During my teenage years, I knew of one person who did not care much for me. She never came up and said, "I hate you," but it was very evident by her actions that she strongly disliked me.

There were also a couple of people during my college years who would write hurtful letters or try to get me into trouble. Now, as I already mentioned, my feelings during those times were not warm and fuzzy toward them. In fact, I felt quite hurt by some of them, and maybe you can understand because you are going through a similar problem right now. To those of you who have or have had someone treat you as if he or she hated you, let me say first of all: you cannot control the person; you can only control you. No matter how hard you try, you will probably never get that person to change how he or she feels about you, but

you can control how you feel about that person.

When someone does not like you, it bothers you, doesn't it? If you are not careful, it can control your mind, and that is exactly what the Devil wants it to do. It can even sometimes cause you to become very unkind and hateful if you let it.

Let's look at a few ways God says we should deal with our feelings toward our enemies.

1. We should pray for the person. Now, this does not mean to pray for something bad to happen to the person or for God to strike him dead! This verse is telling us to pray that God would give the person a good day and bless him or her and help the person to be happy. It's hard to hate someone for whom you are praying!

2. We should forgive the person. To forgive someone doesn't mean you just wake up one morning, ask God to forgive your enemy, and you love that person for the rest of your life. I wish it were that easy. You might need to ask God each day to help you forgive that person who has hurt you. You may need to even ask several times a day. Maybe every time you see or think about the person you need to pray and ask God to help you forgive him or her. This process takes time, but eventually God will give you the forgiveness you need.

3. We should love the person. Love is an action, and in order to love someone, we need to be doing for the person. Praying for the person will give you a love for him or her, but we should look for ways to show kindness and love. Have you ever heard the saying "Kill them with kindness"? Well, that is kind of what we are talking about.

If you are so hurt you cannot be kind to the person who has hurt you, you need to pray for the person, ask for forgiveness, and stay away from the person as much as possible. Once God has begun to help you forgive the person, you can be kind to him or her.

Here are a few simple ideas you can do to help you love your enemies:

- Write a kind, anonymous note.

- Say "hi" when you see the person and smile.

- Tell one of the person's friends something nice about the person.

- Compliment the person when you see him or her.

- Leave an anonymous gift for the person.

I think this is one of the most difficult relationships on which to work, but if you decide to try to forgive that person who has hurt you, God will do the rest. Also, ask God to help you to never make someone else feel hurt or rejected by your words or actions. It is a challenge, but I believe you can truly love your enemies.

CHAPTER ELEVEN

Bind Us Together

I have a great group of Sunday school girls this year. I love their sweet spirits and fun personalities, but I also love how they treat each other.

I had an activity recently, and all we did was take a girl for a makeover. The whole activity was really for one girl to feel beautiful, but seven girls came to watch (and shop) and make her feel like she looked nice.

My dad has been preaching on prayer for the past several months on Sunday nights, so we decided to pray together as a class on a recent Sunday morning. As we were praying, one girl, who goes to a public school, prayed for courage to take a stand; another girl prayed for her dad who lives in Vietnam to be able to come to America with her and her mother; another girl prayed for God to help her mom who lives alone with her two girls because her husband passed away many years ago; others prayed for the salvation of

unsaved relatives and even immediate family members.

My class is a mixture of Christian school girls, public school girls, City Baptist girls (a school for bus kids), and visitors who have never been saved, and what I am impressed with the most is how well they treat each other. There is no mocking or making fun of each other to hurt someone. The Christian school girls are kind and even go out of their way to make the public school girls feel loved and welcomed.

We have a theme this year in our class: "Bind Us Together." I chose this theme because I wanted the girls to become a unit and a team, and they have. There is a great spirit in our room on Sundays, and I appreciate their love and friendship toward me and each other.

In Jude 22 and 23, the Bible says, *"And of some have compassion, making a difference: And others save with fear, pulling them out of the fire; hating even the garment spotted by the flesh."* The first verse talks about treating others with compassion and loving people; the second verse talks about hating sin, yet loving the sinner.

It is so easy to see someone else's failures and faults or their "weird" or "quirky" ways and to poke fun and laugh at them. Every school has its "misfits," as we might call them, or its "not-so-popular" crowd who may just not be quite as "normal" as everyone thinks they should be.

Brother Mike Monte was preaching at one of our youth revivals, and I liked what he said. He told us that everyone is weird in his own way. He said, "At least I know I'm weird, and I admit it; some of you need to realize that you're weird, too. Who cares? Everyone is [different] in his own way, so no one has a right to make fun of others."

Often in life the "misfits" of our schools and neighborhoods become menaces to society as adults because they were constantly ridiculed and made fun of as kids and teenagers. They always stood out no matter how hard they tried to fit in, and they just became tired of trying to be popular and to fit in with those who thought they were better than they.

Many of those people who shoot their teachers and classmates at school or who hurt children and animals do so because they have been hurt themselves. They have never been shown love and compassion; therefore, they do not know how to love.

It is so important for us to respect each other and treat one another with dignity. Every person is a creation of God Almighty. To make fun of one of His creations is to say God made a mistake. Did He make a mistake with you? Sometimes you may feel like He did, but our God makes no mistakes. He has a definite purpose and plan for every person He creates, and that includes you. It also includes that "loser" whom you make fun of over and over again day after day.

In closing, let me just ask you this: Do you treat the "misfits" in your school and youth group like you want to be treated? Are you encouraging someone to do right and love God, or could your classmate be the next one in the news because of a school shooting? If you treat people right, you may be saving not only your life, but also the lives of those around you.

CHAPTER TWELVE

I Like People!

Life is full of relationships, and your ability to get along with the different people in these relationships determines how happy your life will be.

My Aunt Kristi was (and still is) one of my favorite aunts. I loved going to her house because she was so fun to be with. I have many good memories of times we spent together baking cookies, putting together puzzles, swimming, talking, and lots of other things she did to make me feel loved. She was not hard for me to get along with because I always felt like she enjoyed being with me. I enjoyed being with her, and as a result, we had (and still have) a very good relationship. However, I would have to say a few people I have known would not be my favorite people with whom to spend time, and getting along with them was very difficult. I love people, and I try to get along with all of them, but at times it can be very tricky, and as one

famous secular singer once sang, sometimes you have to learn to "tiptoe through the tulips"!

When Paul wrote, *"If it be possible, as much as lieth in you, live peaceably with all men"* (Romans 12:18), Paul did not even know if it was possible to get along with everyone. Yet I think this verse is the key to having successful relationships in your life. The words *"...as much as lieth in you..."* explain that we can do the best we can do; we cannot control how others feel about us or treat us. We can make sure we are right toward them in our heart, and we can be kind to them—no matter how they treat us.

Mrs. Marlene Evans taught me in our college class to give people what they want. Now, often that is hard to do. A girl comes to school one day wearing a new outfit, and she knows she looks good. When she marches up to your locker, tells you where she got it, how much she paid for it, that she lost five pounds and bought two sizes smaller than she usually wears, the last thing you want to tell her is how nice she looks! So instead you say, "I saw Sarah wearing the exact same outfit, and it looked much nicer on her." Then you walk away rolling your eyes.

Solomon said everyone is full of vanity (which is the opposite of humility, by the way), and in order to get along with people, we have to humble ourselves. If we humble ourselves, God will take notice, and we will be able to give people what they want.

Some people in school would tell me the only reason I received this or that was because of who I was. I would consider people who talked that way to be difficult people with whom to get along. What I wanted to do was tell them the reasons why they were wrong and I was right, but that would have gotten us nowhere! All I could do was be kind to them and let them say whatever they wanted to say because whether or not I defended myself, their mouth was not going to stop running. So I decided to save myself the trouble of defending myself, and eventually the person cooled off.

Now I am no saint, and I like to talk, so I am sure there have been people who have been offended by something I said or did to them, and if someone is reading this article and is one of them, I am sorry. My goal, however, is to work on what Paul said, "...*as much as lieth in* (me)," and to do everything in my power to get along with everyone who crosses my path.

I once heard someone say that 99.9% of females are insecure, and let me add that the other .1% are just too insecure to admit it! If you view all people as insecure people who need someone to help them feel loved and accepted, that might help you get along with them better.

That girl in your youth group who is so popular and seems to get along with everyone worries about fitting in just as much (maybe more) than you do. The star on the team who always makes the most points and is the coach's favorite worries if everyone likes him.

If you will try to apply these principles and do everything in your power to get along with people, you will find you will never lack for friends or people who want to hang around you because everyone likes to be around nice people! And how do you become a nice person? You guessed it—give people what they want!

CHAPTER THIRTEEN

Guard Your Heart

*W*e have discussed how to have good relationships with many different people in our lives, but in order to have good relationships in all of these areas, we must first have a good relationship with God, and that means making sure our heart is right with Him. Let's see what the Bible has to say about having a heart that is right with God.

- *"The heart is deceitful above all things, and desperately wicked: who can know it?"* (Jeremiah 17:9)

- *"…for man looketh on the outward appearance, but the LORD looketh on the heart."* (I Samuel 16:7)

- *"My heart is fixed, O God, my heart is fixed: I will sing and give praise."* (Psalm 57:7)

- *"For as he thinketh in his heart, so is he…."*
  (Proverbs 23:7)

- How do you feel when someone says something nice to you or is friendly to you?

- How do you react when someone hurts you deeply or breaks the trust you had placed in him/her?

- What do you want to do when you are falsely accused of something and you know you are innocent?

- How do you feel when an animal is mistreated or a family pet dies?

- What do you think when a child is abused or an elderly person is hurt?

- How do you feel when you do well on a test or get a good report card?

All of those reactions and feelings come from somewhere deep inside you, from a place where no

one sees but you and God, a place where you really live when no one is around, the place you try to hide sometimes from others—your heart.

I love the song called "Guard Your Heart," and the words go like this:

"What appears to be a harmless glance can turn to romance,
And homes are divided;
Feelings that should never have been awakened within
Tearing the heart in two,
Listen I beg of you,

Guard your heart; guard your heart.
Don't trade it for treasure, don't give it away.
Guard your heart; guard your heart.
As a payment for pleasure, it's a high price to pay,
For a soul that remains sincere, with a conscience clear.
Guard your heart."

The Bible says our heart is "desperately wicked," yet "who can know it?" There have been many

graduates from our high school and college who seemed to have it all together in life and looked like the perfect examples of the Christian teenager. Yet, when they graduated, somewhere down the road, we began to see what they were really like. As the Bible says, we cannot see what people are like on the inside; our only evidence is what is shown on the outside.

Some teenage girls from our youth group who were always sweet, smiling, seemingly happy girls have turned out to be hateful, deceitful, lying girls who care only about themselves. How does this happen? Do they just one day wake up and say, "I think I'll be hateful today to everyone"? No, they are just displaying now what they have always been; they did not "guard their heart."

On the other hand, some girls in our teen church for Sunday school bus riders at first seemed like punks, causing trouble and being disrespectful until they saw that we truly loved and cared about them. When they no longer felt threatened and unloved (as they probably do at home), they let down their "mask" of defiance and hatred and began to show what was really in their hearts. Deep down inside, waiting to be opened, was a bottle of love, happiness, and joy. But through the years, those feelings and emotions had been pounded shut over and over through abuse, neglect, and rejection. These girls were not hateful girls; they simply had put up a wall of defense to protect themselves from more hurt and pain.

Satan would like nothing better than to contaminate the hearts of Christian teenage girls with his evil weapons of hatred, lust, envy, greed, and so forth. He uses television, the Internet, movies, music, books, magazines, the mall, billboards, commercials, other teens whose hearts are wicked, a boyfriend; you name it, Satan tries his best to corrupt one's heart. Who can possibly withstand the enemy on his own? By ourselves, we are powerless, but there is good news. Mark 10:27 says, "*...for with God all things are possible.*"

With God, you can have a pure heart.

With God, you can love your enemies.

With God, you can take a stand for right.

With God, you can stay pure to the wedding altar.

With God, you can say "no" to the boyfriend who asks you to be immoral.

With God, you can daily read your Bible and pray.

With God, you can have courage in your public school.

With God, you can guard your heart from the evil one.

Now I want you to take the following test to see if your heart is pure and holy with God. Answer these questions honestly in your heart or on paper, and this will show you if you are guarding your heart.

1. Do you read your Bible on a somewhat daily basis?

2. Are you talking to God on a regular basis and asking for forgiveness of sin?

3. Does the music to which you listen make you feel closer to God?

4. Do you watch an hour or more of television or surf the Internet daily?

5. Do you ever think of or talk about God at school?

6. Do you have an open, honest relationship with your parents?

7. Do you have a cabinet of counselors who help you in every big decision you make, including the choice of the one you date?

8. In your spare time, about what one person or thing do you spend the most time thinking?

If you feel your answers to this little test would be pleasing to God and you would not be embarrassed for your pastor, parents, or friends to see them, then you are on the right track. However, if you would be humiliated for anyone to look at your answers and you know they are not pleasing to God, then you are not guarding your heart. It will not be long before your heart is corrupted. One day those around you will see who you really are.

Ultimately, your relationship with God is the one relationship that will determine the success of all other areas of your life. "*The heart is deceitful above all things,*

and desperately wicked: who can know it?" (Jeremiah 17:9) God does, and so will everyone else one day. He alone can help you to guard it and to keep it with all diligence.

Do you want to have close relationships with your family and friends? It starts with having a pure heart. If your heart is right with God, He will take care of all of your other relationships. If your heart is not right with God, every other relationship you have will suffer. So let me ask you this: If every relationship begins with God, then how is your relationship with Him?